Aone Cursive Writing

Prabhas Rao

Hand and Body Position

If you write with right hand.

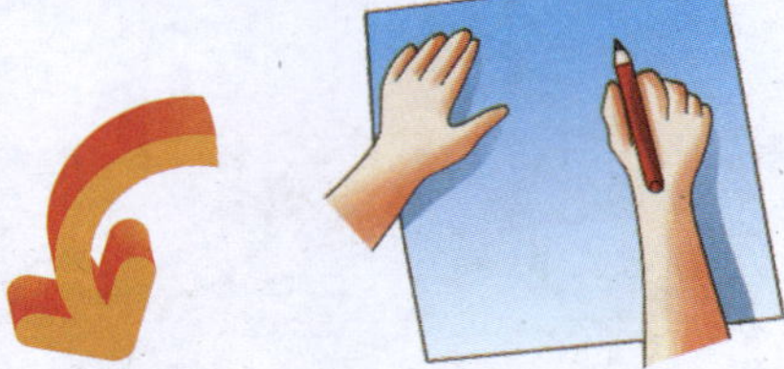

Paper is placed on an angle to the left . Lefthand steadies the paper and moves it up as you near the bottom of the page. Right hand is free to write.

If you write with left hand.

Paper is placed on an angle to the right . Right hand steadies the paper and moves it up as you near the bottom of the page. Left hand is free to write.

Hold the pencil loosely about 1/2 to 1" above the sharpened point. Hold it between your thumb and index (pointer) finger. Let it rest on your middle finger. Do not grip the pencil tightly or your hand will become very tired. Do not let your hand slip down to the sharp point or you will have difficulty in writing properly.

First trace and then copy the given sentences.

Health is wealth. Always try

Health is wealth. Always try

to maintain good health.

to maintain good health.

Always wash your hands before

Always wash your hands before

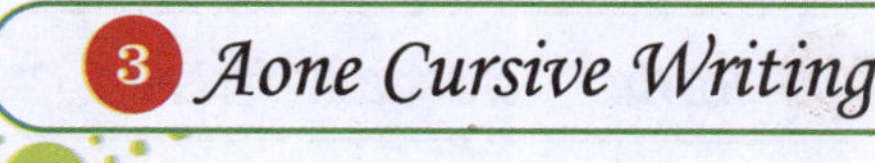

taking your food. Take fresh

taking your food. Take fresh

food. Never take any fruits

food. Never take any fruits

that are cut long before. Uncover

that are cut long before. Uncover

food should be avoided. Never

food should be avoided. Never

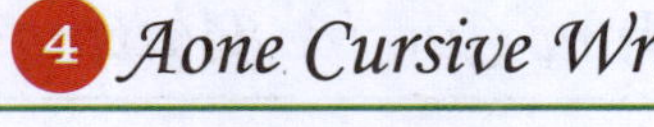

eat too much. Avoid oily and

eat too much. Avoid oily and

rich food. Take physical

rich food. Take physical

exercise regularly. Morning

exercise regularly. Morning

walk is good for health

walk is good for health

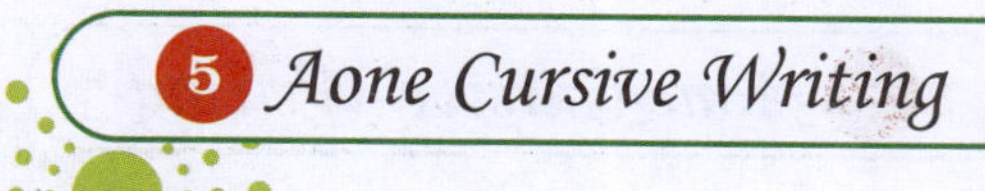

First trace and then copy the given sentences.

Do you know a fish has no

Do you know a fish has no

eyebrow? Do you know a deer

eyebrow? Do you know a deer

can run faster than a tiger?

can run faster than a tiger?

A monkey has no leg. A cow

A monkey has no leg. A cow

has four rooms in its stomach

has four rooms in its stomach

while the other animals have

while the other animals have

only one room in stomach. Do

only one room in stomach. Do

you know a rhinoceros has

you know a rhinoceros has

the thickest skin of all the

the thickest skin of all the

animals? A rattlesnake

animals? A rattlesnake

produces sound when it

produces sound when it

walks. When a bat flies

walks. When a bat flies

it flies backward. A new born

it flies backward. A new born

baby of a bear weighs

baby of a bear weighs

less than 50 gms.

less than 50 gms.

Be ready to know about the tigers. First trace and then copy the given sentences.

Children, who teaches you to

Children, who teaches you to

take bath? Who helps you to

take bath? Who helps you to

eat, swim and to do other

eat, swim and to do other

necessary things? It is your

necessary things? It is your

mom who helps you to do things.

mom who helps you to do things.

The same thing happens to

The same thing happens to

a tiger family. A tigress

a tiger family. A tigress

alone takes all the charges

alone takes all the charges

of its cubs. It guards the cubs.

of its cubs. It guards the cubs.

It feeds the cubs. But these are

It feeds the cubs. But these are

very common. The mother

very common. The mother

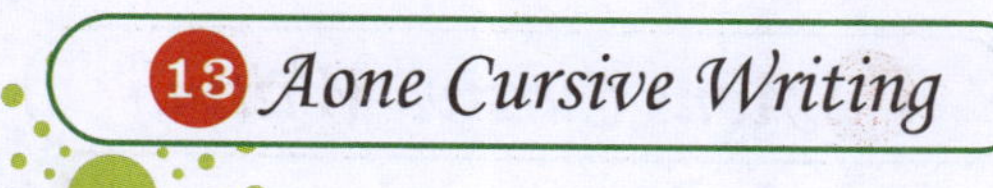

trains her cubs in a way so

trains her cubs in a way so

that they can live in the

that they can live in the

that they can live in the

that they can live in the

meek. The mother trains them

meek. The mother trains them

how to kill prey, how to

how to kill prey, how to

swim etc. At first, the mother

swim etc. At first, the mother

wounds a prey and the cubs

wounds a prey and the cubs

kill it finally. The training of

kill it finally. The training of

swimming is very interesting.

swimming is very interesting.

At first, the mother goes down

At first, the mother goes down

to the water and calls the

to the water and calls the

cubs. But the cubs do not go

cubs. But the cubs do not go

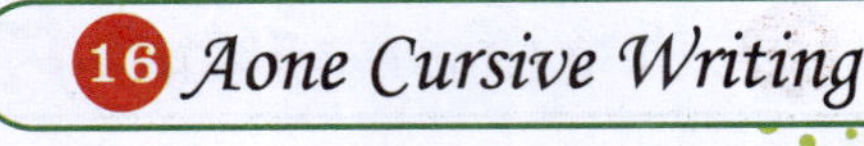

to the water. Then, the mother

to the water. Then, the mother

comes out of water and drags

comes out of water and drags

them to the water.

them to the water.

Now, learn about birds. First trace and then copy the given sentences.

Nightingale bird

Cuckoo bird

Mocking bird

There are many birds those who

There are many birds those who

can sing well. Moreover, they

can sing well. Moreover, they

have sweet voice. Nightiangle

have sweet voice. Nightiangle

and cuckoo are such birds.

and cuckoo are such birds.

These birds have sweet voice.

These birds have sweet voice.

But mocking bird is a different

But mocking bird is a different

type of food. It is clear

type of food. It is clear

from its name that it can

from its name that it can

imitate other's voice. It is slim

imitate other's voice. It is slim

and its size is like a robin.

and its size is like a robin.

It has a sharp beak. The

It has a sharp beak. The

colour of its eyes is yellowish

colour of its eyes is yellowish

orange. Its tone is joyous. It

orange. Its tone is joyous. It

never sings a sad song.

never sings a sad song.

Now, learn about penguins. First trace and then copy the given sentences.

Penguins are the birds and

Penguins are the birds and

these are fond of swimming

these are fond of swimming

instead of flying. A penguin's

instead of flying. A penguin's

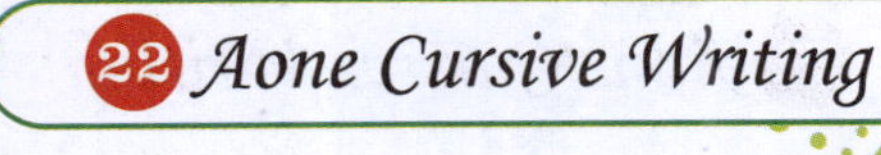

wings are black. Its front

wings are black. Its front

colour is white. It can stand

colour is white. It can stand

and walk on its two feet,

and walk on its two feet,

called flippers. They live

called flippers. They live

in group. When they walk,

in group. When they walk,

they look like lawyers. They

they look like lawyers. They

like to dive, swim and

like to dive, swim and

merrymaking.

merrymaking.

Tiger is our national animal.

Tiger is our national animal.

Tiger is our national animal.

Tiger is our national animal.

Peacock is our national bird.

Peacock is our national bird.

Peacock is our national bird.

Peacock is our national bird.

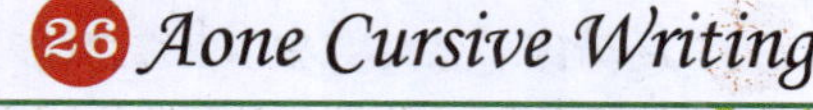

The Qutab Minar is in Delhi.

The Qutab Minar is in Delhi.

The Qutab Minar is in Delhi.

The Qutab Minar is in Delhi.

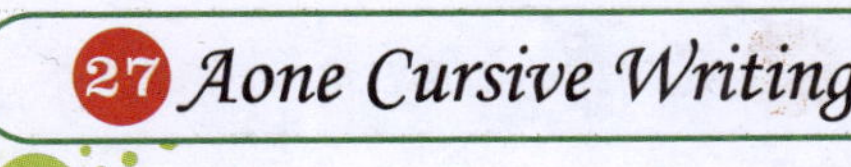

The Taj Mahal is in Agra.

The Taj Mahal is in Agra.

The Taj Mahal is in Agra.

The Taj Mahal is in Agra.

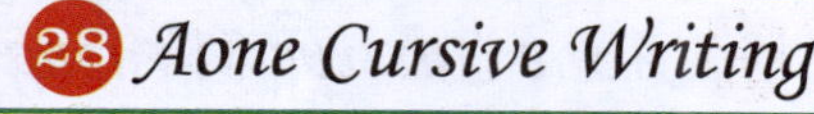

Jaipur is called Pink city.

Jaipur is called Pink city.

Jaipur is called Pink city.

Jaipur is called Pink city.

Kashmir is a beautiful place.

Kashmir is a beautiful place.

Kashmir is a beautiful place.

Kashmir is a beautiful place.

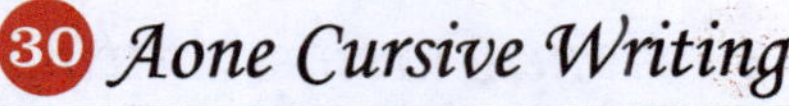

Walking is the best exercise.

Walking is the best exercise.

Walking is the best exercise.

Walking is the best exercise.

Honesty is the best policy.

Honesty is the best policy.

Honesty is the best policy.

Honesty is the best policy.

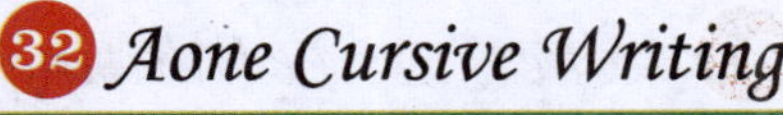

Always respect your parents.

Always respect your parents.

Always respect your parents.

Always respect your parents.

A rainbow has seven colours.

A rainbow has seven colours.

A rainbow has seven colours.

A rainbow has seven colours.

Man makes his opportunities.

Man makes his opportunities.

Man makes his opportunities.

Man makes his opportunities.

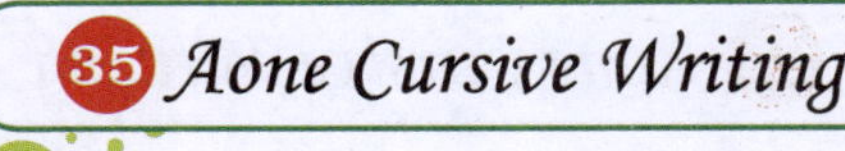

First think then speak.

First think then speak.

First think then speak.

First think then speak.

History is the witness of time.

History is the witness of time.

History is the witness of time.

History is the witness of time.

It is better to late than never.

It is better to late than never.

It is better to late than never.

It is better to late than never.

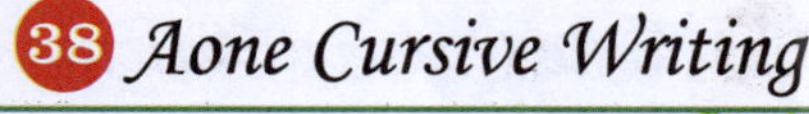

Anger is an enemy of man.

Anger is an enemy of man.

Anger is an enemy of man.

Anger is an enemy of man.

Write something about your school picnic in the lines given below.

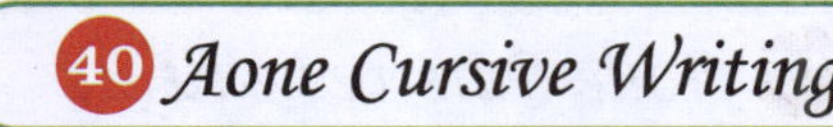